monsters in my closet

But Not for Long!

Written by Becky Fischer

Illustrated by Shannon Wirrenga

Monsters in My Closet
Written by Becky Fischer
Illustrated by Shannon Wirrenga
Cover Artwork by Shannon Wirrenga
Coloring, Layout, Lettering, and Design by Becky Fischer
Angel pg 3 © iStock.com
Pg 12, 13, 15, 25, 18, 28,-37 © Canstockphotos.com

Kids in Ministry International website: www.kidsinministry.org
For information call 701-258-6786 or
Email: kidsinministry@yahoo.com

God has not given us a spirit of fear, but of power, love, and a sound mind. 2 Timothy 1:7

Caleb Harper had a problem. Something bad happened at night when he went to sleep. It didn't happen every night. But it was often enough to make him afraid to go to bed.

Sometimes when he fell asleep he would hear noises in the darkness. The noises would wake him up. They sounded like voices talking to him saying scary, mean things.

When he slowly opened his eyes he saw something that looked like monsters in his closet. It was awful! Sometimes they would have horns, a tail, sharp teeth, and an evil laugh. Their laugh sounded like something he had heard on one of his favorite cartoon shows.

Caleb would shut his innocent brown eyes tightly, pull the blanket over his head, and cry. The problem was no one could see the monsters but him. Caleb was very afraid!

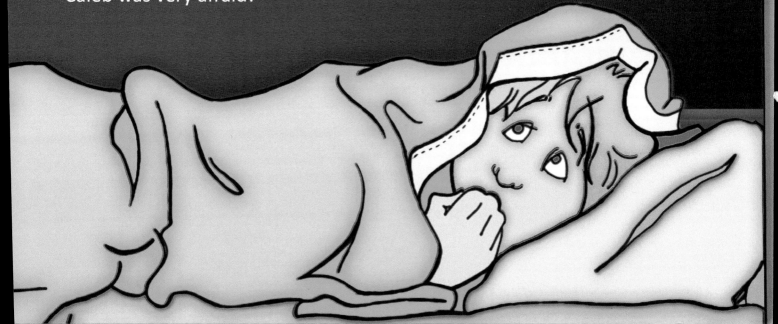

"Mommy! Mommy!" Caleb would yell in the darkness when the monsters came. There were other times he was so scared he couldn't say a word.

"There are monsters in my closet!"

"It's okay, Caleb," his mother comforted him.

Mr. Harper would walk over to the closet, open the door, and say, "There's nothing there, Caleb."

"But, Daddy, I saw them! You believe me, don't you?"

"Yes, I do, son. I just don't know how to help."

Then his mom and dad would hold him tightly and pray for him until the fear went away.

"Repeat this after me, Caleb," Mrs. Harper would say as she cuddled him. "God has not given me a spirit of fear, but of power, love and a sound mind!"

Caleb obeyed, "God has not given me a spirit of fear, but of power, love and a sound mind!"

He obediently said it, but it didn't always come from his heart.

Because his parents didn't know how to help their son any more, Caleb's dad called their church and asked their pastor, David, to come and talk with them.

"It's very important not to allow anything in our homes or in our lives that would be an open invitation to these unwanted visitors," Pastor David explained.

"Without realizing it, we can open doors to the enemy. Then these monsters, as you call them, come into our homes and our lives, and cause us all kinds of unwelcome problems."

"We don't have any enemies. What enemy are you talking about, Pastor? " Mrs. Harper asked.

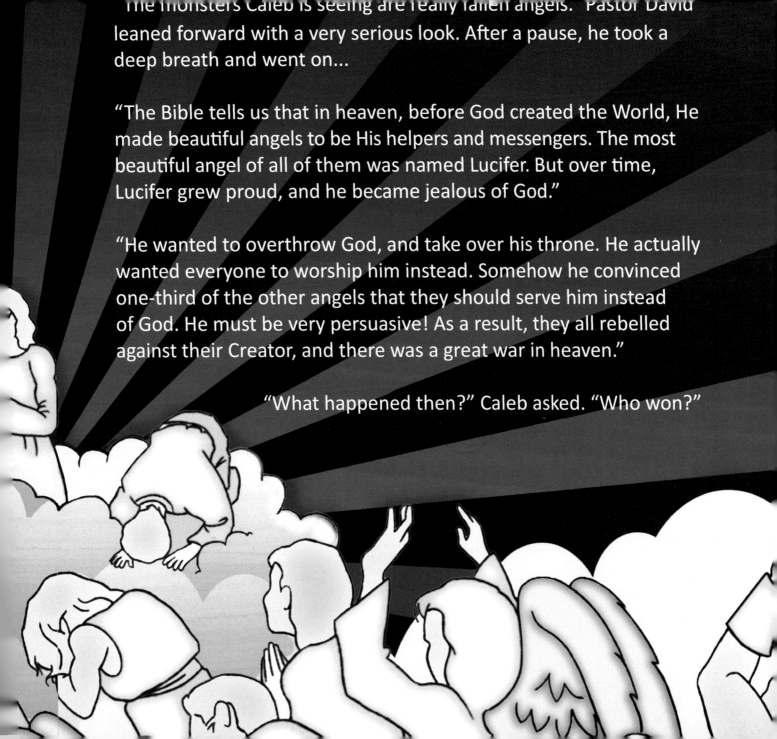

The monsters Caleb is seeing are really fallen angels. Pastor David leaned forward with a very serious look. After a pause, he took a deep breath and went on...

"The Bible tells us that in heaven, before God created the World, He made beautiful angels to be His helpers and messengers. The most beautiful angel of all of them was named Lucifer. But over time, Lucifer grew proud, and he became jealous of God."

"He wanted to overthrow God, and take over his throne. He actually wanted everyone to worship him instead. Somehow he convinced one-third of the other angels that they should serve him instead of God. He must be very persuasive! As a result, they all rebelled against their Creator, and there was a great war in heaven."

"What happened then?" Caleb asked. "Who won?"

"Lucifer and the fallen angels were no match for God, Caleb. Only the Most High God is all powerful, and all knowing.

The powers and abilities Lucifer and his fallen angels have are very limited by comparison. Even though Lucifer and friends tried, their supernatural powers (which are really magic powers in disguise) didn't even come close to the power of God! Our heavenly Father had no choice but to kick them all out of heaven!"

Pastor David leaned back, tapped his Bible with his finger, and said, "From that point on in the Word, Lucifer got a new name. He became known as Satan, and the fallen angels were called demons, or devils."

"What does this have to do with the monsters in my closet?" Caleb asked.

"When Satan saw how much God loved people, he became very jealous of them. Since he failed to overthrow God in heaven, he tried to hurt Him in a different way. That old snake began to take his hatred out on people, especially innocent little boys and girls because he knew how special they were to God."

"One of the things he does is try to scare them and fill them with fear just like he has been doing to you." Then Pastor David smiled. "They don't want you to know that you have power over them in the name of Jesus!"

"But by allowing the wrong kinds of books, DVDs, video games, and music into our homes and hearts that talk about evil things, we blindly invite the enemy right in! We have to be careful to only allow things in our homes and our hearts that glorify and honor Jesus."

From that point on Caleb's parents made the decision not to let their son watch any movies, TV shows, or cartoons that had scary things in them, especially things like magic, witchcraft, or ghosts.

They were very careful what music they allowed Caleb to listen to. They even became very strict about the books their son was allowed to read. Anything that had magic, witchcraft, ghosts, casting spells, superhuman powers, and similar things, were absolutely off limits!

They carefully went through their home and threw away anything they thought might be an open door to the monsters.

"Tonight before you go to bed, Caleb," Pastor David had told the Harpers, "I would like for you to take some oil. Oil is a symbol of the Holy Spirit. You, your mom, and dad are to dip your fingers in the oil, and smear some over everything in your room. This includes the windows, doors, the furniture, your bed, and even your toys."

"What then?" Mr. Harper asked.

"As you do this, each of you need to pray out loud and ask God to fill Caleb's room with his holy angels. Invite the presence of the Holy Spirit to come in and stay there," Pastor David instructed. "Then let Satan and his friends know they are no longer welcome in Caleb's room ever again. From now on this is where there presence of God lives."

"One last thing," Pastor David stood up to leave. "When it's time for Caleb to go to sleep, turn on some soft worship music that glorifies Jesus. Let it play all night long. Satan and those monsters hate it when we worship God."

Caleb and his mom and dad did exactly what Pastor David told them to do. For several weeks Caleb slept peacefully and without any ugly, night time visitors.

Then one night, without warning, the monsters were back! When Caleb woke up, the fear was so strong he could hardly breathe!

They were laughing at him from the corner of his room. Caleb screamed out in fear. His parents came running to see what was wrong.

"There they are, Daddy, right there!" Caleb pointed to the corner as he cried and shook uncontrollably.

Mr. and Mrs. Harper could not see anything, but it was obvious Caleb could. Caleb's dad raised his arm and pointed his finger at the corner. "Devil, you leave my son alone in the name of Jesus! He is protected by the power of the blood of Jesus! Go now, in Jesus' name!"

Caleb breathed a sigh of relief and grabbed his dad. Holding him tightly he whispered in his ear, "He's gone, daddy." Then he begged his parents to let him sleep in their room the rest of the night.

Caleb's parents called Pastor David to come over again.

"We've done everything you told us to do, Pastor, and we made a lot of progress," Mr. Harper reported. "So why did the monsters come back again?"

"One big reason," the pastor explained, "is just because they are stubborn, and they don't want to go. So they test you." The pastor sat quietly for a minute like he was thinking. Then he looked at Caleb.

"Caleb, have you ever asked Jesus to forgive your sins and come into your heart to be your Lord and savior?"

Caleb quietly shook his head, "No."

"This is something that is very important to do. We become children of God when we do this. The Holy Spirit actually moves into our hearts, and lives on the inside of us. This gives us much more power over the Enemy. It's not because of us, but because of Jesus inside of us." Pastor David's eyes twinkled when he talk-ed.

The little boy became excited about asking Jesus to come and live inside of Him. He prayed with Pastor David asking Jesus to forgive his sins, and come into his heart.

"Things are different now, Caleb. Jesus has always loved you and wanted to protect you. But from this day on he can help you from the inside out!" The friendly pastor gave him a big hug. "You have authority over the monsters that you didn't have before!"

"What is authority?" the child asked.

"It means you're the boss now over all the monsters because of Jesus on the inside of you. It's just like a policeman who has authority over criminals. Only our authority comes from God Himself.

"So the next time the monsters come, it's okay to call mom and dad if you want to. But from now on *you* are the one that needs to tell the monsters to go. Tell them to leave in the name of Jesus!"

Pastor David gave Caleb a high five and turned to leave.

Sure enough, a couple of nights later the ugly monsters came back again. This time it was so awful it was like a heavy blanket of fear that filled Caleb's room.

When he could catch his breath, Caleb screamed in fright, and once again his parents came running in. Caleb was standing on his bed pointing to the same corner. He was trembling from head to foot. This was the worst it had ever been!

Caleb's dad automatically turned to command the monsters to leave like he had done before. But just as he started to speak, he stopped. He remembered what Pastor David had told them.

"Caleb, you have to do it," dad looked at his son with firmness. "You are the one who has to tell those monsters to leave this time! They need to hear it from you!"

Caleb was still full of fear. He looked at the monsters. They were laughing and pointing at him. They were making him feel scared and ashamed.

"Caleb, you have to say it!" Dad was insistent. He kept his eyes on his trembling son.

Caleb could barely get the words out of his mouth. But finally he spoke. "Monsters," he said timidly at first. But then he began to feel boldness rise in his heart. "Jesus lives in my heart now! So you leave me alone! God has given me authority over you. Get out of here and don't come back, in Jesus' name!"

By the time he finished, Caleb's fear was completely gone! He felt a boldness he had never experienced before! Out of the corner of his eye he saw a huge, brilliantly glowing angel standing next to him. He was so tall his head touched the ceiling! He was ten times bigger than the monsters!

All of a sudden, the slimey beasts fell to the floor and began to shrink. They were shaking in fear. They looked like comical cartoon characters he had seen on TV. It was actually a very funny sight.

The monsters looked so silly and hilarious that Caleb burst out laughing. The giant angel laughed with him. When Caleb looked at the cowering, shriveled up little demons, he wondered why he had ever been afraid of him in the first place.

Mr. and Mrs. Harper couldn't see the angel or the monsters. But seeing Caleb laughing hard made them start laughing too!

"Caleb, this is what happens when you take authority over monsters in the name of Jesus." The angel glowed filling the room with his brilliant, warm light. He spoke with a voice that was loud, commanding, and powerful. "Demons tremble at the name of Jesus! They are afraid of Him, and because He lives in you, they are afraid of you too!"

The fear in Caleb's heart was completely gone! It had burst like a balloon and disappeared. That was the last time Caleb ever saw his ugly, smelly, unwanted visitors. Now he knew that he never had to be afraid of any monster ever again. Because of Jesus living inside of him, he had more power than any monster!

The End

Extra Notes for Mom & Dad

Although the story of little Caleb and the monsters in the previous pages is make believe, the individual elements in the tale have been experienced by untold thousands of real children. Many people have written to me and shared their personal stories, or their children's. They have experienced, not just typical nightmares that are associated with childhood, but night terrors. Night terrors are unique in many ways. It was from their individual testimonies I molded Caleb's story.

Spiritual vs. Natural Causes

It is important to note that, as with many things that may appear spiritual in nature at first, there can be, and often is, a natural, or even medical explanation. Night terrors (aka sleep terrors) by definition are a sleep disorder in which a person quickly wakes from sleep in a terrified state. It is very easy to find credible medical help on the internet through websites like kidshealth.org, mayoclinic.org, webmd.org, and others for further information. Please take time to research what they have to say to see if it applies to your child.

The general consensus of these organizations is that night terrors happen during deep non-REM sleep. Unlike nightmares (which occur during REM sleep), a night terror is not technically a dream, but more like a sudden reaction of fear that happens during the transition from one sleep phase to another.

Night terrors usually occur about two or three hours after a child falls asleep, when sleep transitions from the deepest stage of non-REM sleep to lighter REM sleep, a stage where dreams occur. This transition is usually a smooth one. But on occasion a child becomes agitated and frightened — and that fear reaction is a night terror.

Contributing Factors

During a night terror, a child might suddenly sit upright in bed and shout out, or scream, in distress. The child's breathing and heartbeat might be faster. He or she might sweat, thrash around, and act upset and scared. After a few minutes, or sometimes longer, a child simply calms down and returns to sleep. Various factors can contribute to sleep terrors, including:

- Sleep deprivation
- Fatigue
- Stress
- Anxiety
- Fever (in children)
- Sleeping in unfamiliar surroundings
- Lights or noise

Sleep terrors can be caused from use of alcohol, illegal drugs, or certain medications including some antihistamines, sedatives, and sleeping pills. Any of these can trigger sleep terror episodes. Sometimes they are associated with underlying conditions that affect sleep, such as:

- Sleep-disordered breathing — a group of disorders characterized by abnormal breathing patterns during sleep, the most common of which is obstructive sleep apnea
- Migraines
- Head injuries

A Real Life Example

One Christian mother of a two and a half year old girl wrote me. The child was apparently was having these type of diagnosable night terrors. She wrote, "Lately, it seems like Anna (not her real name) has been having night terrors frequently. She wakes up all through the night crying and screaming. Sometimes she can't be comforted until she finally wakes up. Sometimes she can't talk and will just sit there, eyes closed and crying. She doesn't respond if I try to hold her or talk to her.

"The last time I tried taking her out of bed and patting her on the back to wake her up. That didn't work. I started praying for her in Jesus' name for it to stop. That didn't work. I tried rocking her. Nothing worked, so I put her back in bed and had to close the door and leave the room, as I didn't know what else to do. When she woke up and calmed down I tried asking her if she was having a bad dream. I don't know if she understands what bad dreams are yet, but she said a bad guy was coming into the house, though she didn't see him now.

"I talked to her about talking to Jesus when she's having a bad dream, and that Jesus is with her even in her dreams. But I don't know how much she understands. When I prayed it didn't help. I pray for her every night to sleep well, and it's not helping. So I'm not sure if this is spiritual or not, but I'm wondering if you have any advice."

A Quick and Easy Solution

In this case, the mother soon found a simple solution through her own efforts. A few days later she wrote again, "Last night I put lavender oil on her pillow and that helped her sleep the rest of the night. Tonight

I put the lavender on her pillow again. She hasn't awakened once so far. We also have Christian nursery songs playing the whole night, and she likes that. I'll keep in touch if I find things that work for her, in addition to prayer, of course."

Again, a few days later, "We have been playing Christian music throughout the night and that seemed to cut down on a lot of waking up. She hasn't had night terrors since I wrote you. The past 3 nights have been amazing. The reason for that is we moved Ellen (her baby sister) into Anna's room. Anna told me she isn't scared because Ellen is in her room. They have both been sleeping beautifully through the night, which is incredible for us. Not only do my husband and I have our room back, but we can get a full night's rest. So I think Anna's waking up at night had to do with feeling alone and scared, because all three of us were in one room, and she was in her own room all by herself."

So in Anna's case, it seemed to be the classical, clinical episodes of night terrors. We recommend you consider getting counsel from your family doctor and take their practical advice to see if your child improves just through taking some natural, common sense steps.

A Notable Difference

However, there is one thing in my brief layman's research that stood out as very different between what the doctors say and what other people, who have shared their experiences with me, have been through. This may be a factor in deciding whether the night terror a child is experiencing is physical or medical in nature, or an actual spiritual issue, as was the case in the story of Caleb.

According to the medical profession, while children often remember nightmares, they won't have any memory of a night terror the next day. Because they were in deep sleep when it happened, there are no actual mental images to recall.

This has definitely not been the case with the people I have communicated with. They have very vivid recall, in great terrifying detail, of their experiences. Shauna D. wrote, "I dreamt of demons chasing me, violent murders, and being taunted by demons. I even got a bird's eye view of hell with demons floating around me. One told me it wanted me to become a habitual liar. I was even physically assaulted by demons." *(More than one person has told me [Becky] the same thing about being physically assaulted in a variety of sinister ways.)* She continued, "I would wake up physically drained and exhausted, sometimes sweating. It was not just a dream. It was all very real."

Terrifying Experiences from Real People

Tina G. wrote, "It actually runs in my family. For at least three or four generations all the women had nightmare and closet monsters as children. I was afraid of the dark until my late teens and remember as a child waking in the morning with marks on my sides or back. *(An example of the physical assaults mentioned above.)* When my own daughter began to have night terrors, I not only came against it in the Name of Jesus, I prayed and fasted to break the generational curse that caused it. She has never had fear at night again, and I know her children will not either."

Catherine J. remembers, "As young as one or two, and until I was in my early twenties, I suffered from these so called night terrors. To describe them is almost impossible because there were rarely dreams attached to them. It was like being plugged into a socket with shock waves going through my body. Indescribable fear surrounded me, and it was always a struggle to wake up. Once I was awake, I did everything in my power to not fall asleep again for fear it would start over."

Devon H. shared, "Growing up, I didn't realize what was happening. But after becoming a Christian as an adult, I put two and two together. I would always have recurring nightmares, and always at the same point in the dream, I would wake up and experience extremely intense fear. I knew there was something in my dark room that was doing this, but I could not see it. I had no way of dealing with this as a kid, so it terrified me. I was terrified of the dark as well."

From Childhood to Teenage Years

Ana M. told me, "This hits hard for me. I have a lot of memories of being tormented as a child and into my teen years. I was afraid of the dark up until probably nineteen or so, when I began to take authority in Jesus' name. My mom remembers, too. I would tell her I saw monsters with tails, horns, and sharp teeth. It sounds silly, but it was true. I remember being fourteen and constantly seeing 'an angel' in the corner of the living room for weeks. Although it looked okay, it had an angry face. I was taught by my Pastor to tell it to leave in Jesus' name, and it did. I accepted Jesus into my heart at fourteen."

Elisa S. said, "I remember night terrors as a child. My parents would pray over me and it would go. But it was like thousands of ants in my mind, almost like the fuzz from old TV's, but in my mind. I was awake, but incapable of controlling it. I was pretty young then—maybe two. At four years old I was filled with the Holy Spirit in children's church. I never dealt with it again like that. There have been a few times in my adulthood when I was under tremendous stress, and I would get small attacks that were similar. I just told them to go in Jesus' name and they left fairly quickly."

As you can see, there seems to be a distinct difference between the experiences of these people and the clinical night terrors where children have no later memory of it. For these people it was much more than going from one sleep phase to the next. You, as the parent, will have to determine which one your child is experiencing and deal with it accordingly. We encourage you to explore all of the natural causes before making an assumption there's something deeper involved.

Power in the Name of Jesus

The most encouraging thing to note is these people eventually were either born again, filled with the spirit, or both, and also learned their authority in the powerful name of Jesus. This is what our make-believe hero, Caleb, learned. He found out eventually he was the one who had to take his authority over the monster (demon) as a child of God. Mom and dad could not always do it for him.

Shauna became equipped with the knowledge that she could call on the Name of Jesus. from a pastor in a little church they attended, even though she was not saved at the time. "I would be gripped in some form of night terror, but even in the dreams, I would begin to call on Jesus, and He would help me to fight."

She eventually received Jesus into her heart and the Lord showed her in a dream to "pray each night and turn my 'dream' life over to Him. He showed me, basically, the demons had an invisible line they just could not cross because of Jesus. I could see them, and they could see me, but they could not get to me. When I realized this, all fear was gone."

She continued, "Now I have children of my own--an eight year old daughter and a four year old son. I do not hide the fact from them that there are angels and demons. They are even more aware that they have a great big Daddy God and Jesus is the biggest superhero ever. They are also aware they might be small, but the Holy Spirit inside of them is not. They understand they are royalty and have authority as sons and daughters of the Most High God." She has taught her children how to rebuke the enemy in Jesus' name.

Authority over a Whimpering Demon

Catherine J. shared, " After becoming a Christian, I found out I could stand on God's word against anything that was not from him. So I started saying the only scripture I knew regarding fear at that time, 'God has not given me a spirit of fear but of power love and a sound mind.' (2 Timothy 1:7)

"It did not seem to be working, however, and these attacks kept on for about two or three months more. Then one night, after one of the worst episodes I had ever had, I woke up speaking this scripture out loud. It was like fear was a thick blanket in my room. Then, all of a sudden, I had a vision of a very demonic being laying on the ground. But he had his arm up over his head as if trying to protect himself. He was whimpering like he was afraid of me!

"I realized at that moment God was showing me how defeated anything demonic was in my life and what demons looked like as we took authority over them. I started laughing, and the fear just burst and disappeared. That was the end of those demonic attacks, which used to occur three or four times a week, many times in one night. Later, every once in a while, usually after I shared my testimony with someone, it would happen again. But I could just laugh or stand against it, and it would stop immediately."

Our Great Big God!

Eric B. shared, "My oldest had night terrors. We felt helpless and sometimes let her scream because if we touched or spoke to her it got 10 times worse. After prayer and a couple of years, they stopped. She also had an awake encounter with a demon in her bedroom when she was very young. It stayed in the corner and she could see it. She would scream and point at it. We were with her but could see nothing. We pointed at the space and told it to go in the name of Jesus. A few days later, she had an awake encounter with Jesus! She came out of her bedroom with so much joy and described in detail where he was and how BIG he was. She said, "He was over me," and pointed up high."

34

It is completely appropriate for you as parents to pray for your children to have dreams and encounters with God to show them His power over the enemy. There are many who believe the reason some children have these experiences is because they have God-given abilities in the realm of the prophetic that He wants to use for His glory. The enemy also knows this (they seem to be able to recognize children who are prophetic, and target them). This is their way of trying to destroy the gift God put in them and keep them from being effective in the Kingdom of God. In other teachings of mine I go into great detail explaining how this generation is the "Joel 2:28 Generation" that the Holy Spirit has had His people prophesying about for centuries. This is the generation God has been waiting for to pour His glory through in the earth. And the devil is trying to make some of them afraid of these experiences so they will not be open to the voice of the Holy Spirit.

Wetting the Bed from Fear

Jessica wrote, "I did not get saved until my son was four. I attribute my sin and open doors to unclean spirits to what my son experienced. I had to learn for his sake how to 'clean house.' I learned to pray with authority, and taught him to do the same.

"One by product of the night terrors," Jessica continued, "was that my son would wet the bed. This was a torment in itself to a young boy who was too old to be experiencing this at the age of 8-9. But God delivered him as we sought the Lord! My son would also describe to me how he heard evil laughs, like are common in Scooby Doo cartoons. So we got rid of all Scooby Doo materials."

Many cartoons today are full of witchcraft, magic, casting spells, and other paranormal activity. They should be avoided completely. There are only two sources of supernatural power. Any magical or supernatural powers that do not come from God, are coming from the devil. So teach your children to avoid them.

Jessica continued, "He learned to come to my bedside and ask for prayer, finding comfort in the words I spoke in the name of Jesus. 'Demons flee at the name of Jesus!' These words, and others, I spoke to my son as I ran to his room to rescue him again and again from the time he was maybe three to four until he was about eight or nine. I would pray things like 'I rebuke you in the name of Jesus!' I would pray for God's angels to watch over him and protect him. It was a persistent battle and a persistent effort of teaching him how to take authority that brought us to the question at the age of eight or nine, 'Have you asked Jesus into your heart? I think this will help you.' So we prayed together and he asked Jesus into his heart with great readiness. My son has not had one bad dream since this time in his life. Now, at age seventeen, God gives him spiritual dreams. Demons are real, but God is real too and God really delivers!"

Salvation and the Baptism in the Holy Spirit

As you minister with your children, note that many times it takes time and persistence, because the enemy does not give up easily. Remember also that leading your child to salvation in Jesus Christ, and also being filled with the Holy Spirit are some of the most powerful weapons God gives us for spiritual warfare. In our story, Caleb found it necessary to ask Jesus into his heart. This was the case with every person who shared their testimonies with me. Still others learned to use the power of worship, by playing Christian worship music in their rooms or their children's rooms. Praise stills the avenger.

Conclusion

In summary, if you have determined that your child's situation is not being caused by some natural or medical reason, then let's discuss what we have learned from our story of Caleb and the experiences of people who wrote to me. If you, as a parent, will take the necessary steps below, there is surely deliverance at the door for your child. God has given weapons of warfare that have ultimate power over the enemy.

1.   Make sure you, your spouse, all of your children, and anyone else living in your home "cleans house' of any books, magazines, comic books, movies, cartoons on TV, video games, card games, music, or anything else that may not be pleasing to the Holy Spirit. Things that are even mildly sexually explicit, and anything with magic and witchcraft it them are an absolute open invitation to the demonic realm.

This would also include any icons, statues, replicas, books, or Dvds, etc of any religions other than Christianity, such as Buddhism, Hinduism, New Age, Islam and more. Any religion that is not based on the saving power of Jesus Christ and Him crucified, and proclaims Him to be the Son of the Living God is a false religion and is opposed to the teachings of the Bible. Any statues of Buddha, Ouija boards, any New Age materials, such as Crystals and magnets, even horoscopes, need to go. Any religious items that do not glorify Jesus Christ are to be expelled from your home.

These things in your home or on your property give demonic spirits a "legal right" to harass and interfere in the lives of your family members in a variety of ways. Some ways may be obvious, like Caleb's night terrors. Other ways are much more subtle and not so obvious, and may take many years before it's clear what problems have come from them. But they are just as lethal in the end. Clean house. Keep in mind the enemy almost always goes after the most vulnerable and helpless--our children.

2.   Lead your child to a saving knowledge of Jesus Christ and as soon as possible begin teaching them about the baptism in the Holy Spirit. Create a hunger in them to be filled and to speak in tongues. The Holy Spirit was given to us for power, authority, and boldness. Praying in tongues is a powerful spiritual weapon.

3.   Teach your child the importance of studying and reading the Bible, even if they aren't old enough to read yet. You read to them from a child's Bible. They, like us, need to soak and renew our minds to the Word of God. Don't get legalistic about it. Rather teach your child to enjoy and love reading the Words of Life.

4.   Teach your child that he or she had authority in the name of Jesus. The Bible says, "Every knee shall bow and every tongues will confess that Jesus Christ is Lord." That includes demons and the powers of darkness. Practice with them and teach them to say phrases like, "Go, in the name of Jesus!" "Leave me alone in Jesus name." The smallest child of God has power and authority over the biggest demon in hell. But they have to be taught to believe this.

5.   Don't get discouraged, and don't give up. Remember the testimonies of the parents who battled, in some cases, for years before they got total victory. Don't believe for one minute that your prayers aren't working. Remember the prophet Daniel in the Old Testament. He prayed for twenty-one days, and later found out that God had dispatched in angels from the minute Daniel started praying. But there was warfare in the heavenlies that was trying to stop them from bringing the answer to his prayers.

Be Encouraged

Remember the victory is yours and your child's in Jesus Christ! This will be one of the greatest learning experiences of your child's spiritual life. It will teach him the things he needs to avoid in order to walk in victory. It will teach him to depend on Jesus. It will teach him the power of the Word, the power of praise, the power in Jesus' name, and so much more. Be sure to write and let us know your testimony. We're trusting God for your child's complete victory!

Becky Fischer
Kids in Ministry International

Scriptures for Your Child to Read and Memorize

God has not given us a spirit of fear, but of power, love, and a sound mind. 2 Timothy 1:7

I have given you authority to trample on snakes and scorpions and to overcome all the power of the enemy; nothing will harm you. Luke 10:19 *(Snakes and scorpions refer to demons and monsters.)*

And these signs will accompany those who believe: In my name they will drive out demons; they will speak in new tongues. Mark 16:17

No weapon formed against me shall prosper. Isaiah 54:17

He gives sleep to the one He loves. Psalm 127:2

Psalms 91 - *(This entire chapter deals with fear and danger. Read from the Bible together.)*

At the name of Jesus every knee should bow, in heaven and on earth and under the earth. Philippians 2:10

Made in the USA
Columbia, SC
12 June 2020